Baxter's Book of MACHINES

by Leon Baxter

COLLINS

All about machines

This book is all about machines. There are useful machines and useless machines – some that might have been and some machines that could never be. Can you join in with the drawing and colouring and make some pictures of your own?

Below are some little pictures with instructions at the side. They are symbol pictures which you will spot throughout the book. When you see them, follow their instruction.

First published in 1989 in the UK by Wm Collins Sons & Co Ltd, 8 Grafton Street, London W1X 3LA
in association with Belitha Press Limited, 31 Newington Green, London N16 9PU
Text and illustrations in this format copyright © Leon Baxter 1989
Art Director: Treld Bicknell   Editor: Carol Watson
All rights reserved. No part of this publication may be reproduced in any form whatsoever without the permission of the publishers and the copyright holders.
ISBN 0 00 191225 9
Printed in Hong Kong for Imago Publishing

 Do some drawing of your own.

 Now you draw in the space provided.

 Now colour the picture.

 Finish this drawing.

18th Century
Dutch Bellows Boat

Some machines look like people.

This car looks like its owner.

This lady looks like her car.

Who drives this car?

The first machines

Long ago people started to invent machines because they wanted to make their lives easier.

This man invented the cart, but it didn't go very fast.

His friend suggested putting wheels on the cart. He tried square ones to begin with . . .

but found round ones were better.

Later they had the first traffic accident,

and the first mechanic appeared.

One day a man needed to lift an ox.

His wife invented the lever, but that didn't work.

Then she invented the fulcrum, but that was no good.

So she put the two together. The ox was lifted, and her husband was very grateful.

Gathering the crops was hard work and took a long time until the invention of the first combine harvester.

Which machine makes your life easier? Can you draw it?

Making machines move

Here is a Lumsden Road-laying Machine ready to start.

Switch it on.

Now the engine is running, and the wheels spin and become a blur.
The exhaust pipe smokes, lines bend, and shake lines appear.

Off we go! As the machine moves forward, the wheels change shape and everything leans forward.

Can you invent your own machine?

Bottling machines

Here are two banana-bottling machines. Can you spot the differences between them? (There are **25**!)

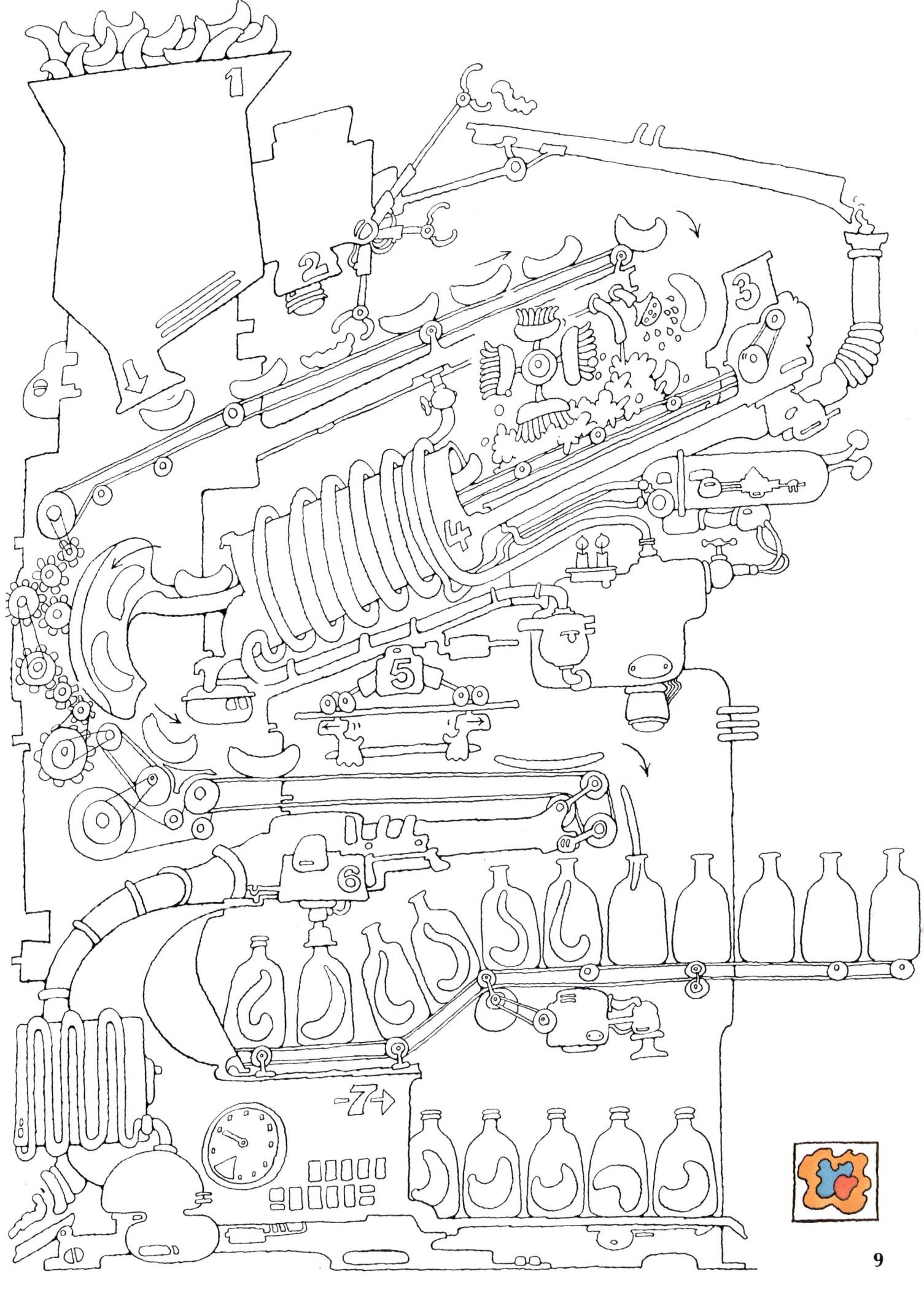

Early flying machines

The first helicopter was built in 1473. It was powered by a perpetual waterfall. It had only one problem – it could only fly upwards. On its first flight it flew straight up into the sky and was never seen again!

Can you design a better flying machine?

In 1689 a Frenchman named Alphonse d'Apht glued lots of candles and a propeller to his hat. The rising hot air made the propeller spin around, and he flew up into the air.

The flight suddenly came to an end when a candle fell over and his hat burst into flames.

Printing

One day a man sat on a plate that had just been painted. Then he sat on a clean unpainted plate. He and his bottom had invented printing.

The First Printing Machine

This made plate painting much faster but gave the man a sore bottom.

The man decided to cut a design into a piece of wood so that only the raised surface would pick up the colour.

You can print like this too.

Slice a potato in half and cut a design in it.

Press it into your paint.

Now you can print.

This man had the idea to cut his design on a log.

By using a long sheet of paper, he could print a repeating pattern.
When he hung the paper up to dry, he found that he had invented wallpaper.

Here is an early wind-driven printing machine.

I have drawn the printing machine.
Can you draw the windmill attached to it?

The Super-grow Ray Gun

Professor Weirdow decided he wanted more hair, so he created a super-grow ray gun to treat his head.

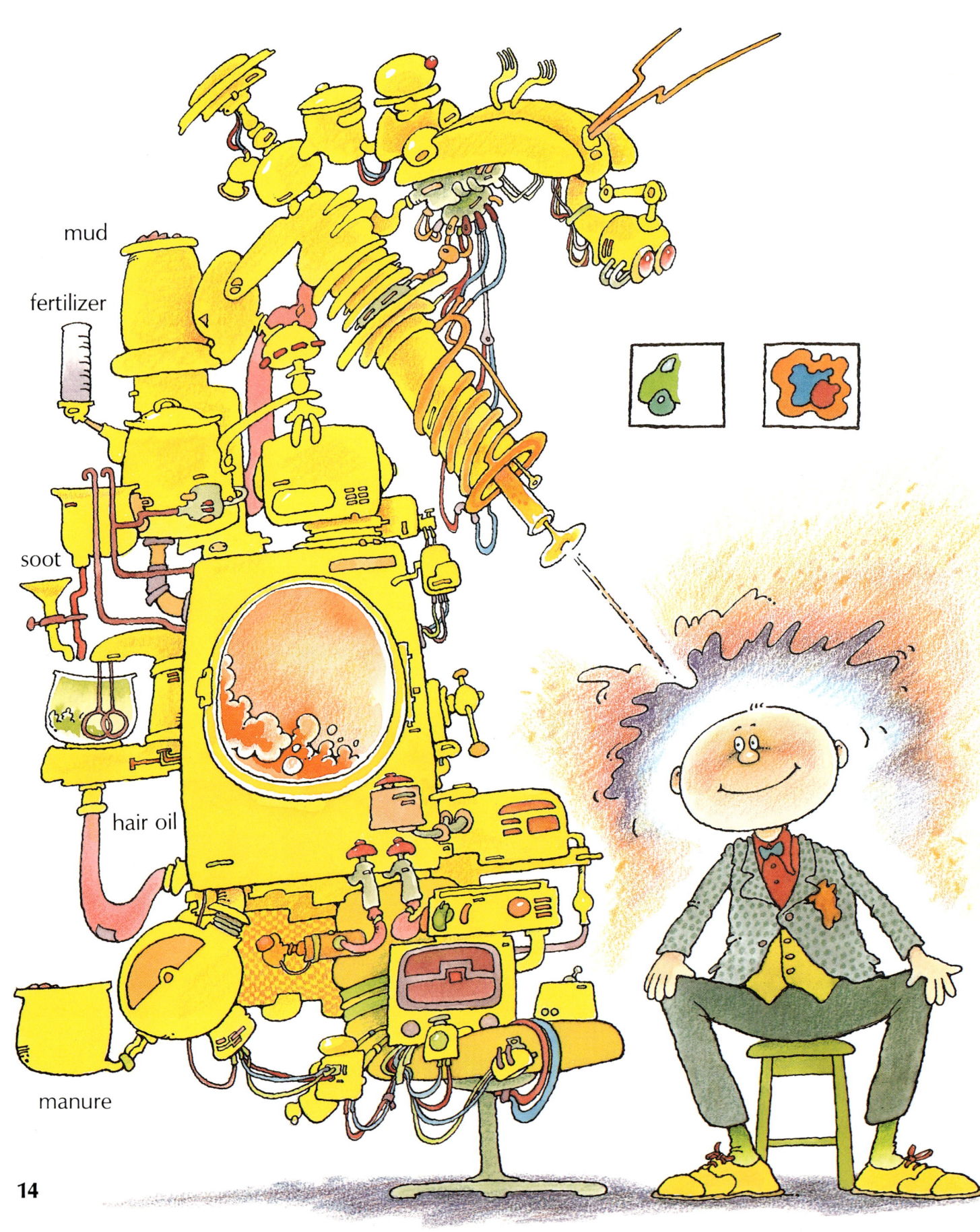

Professor Weirdow switched on his machine and waited for something to happen.

He turned bright green and his ears grew larger.

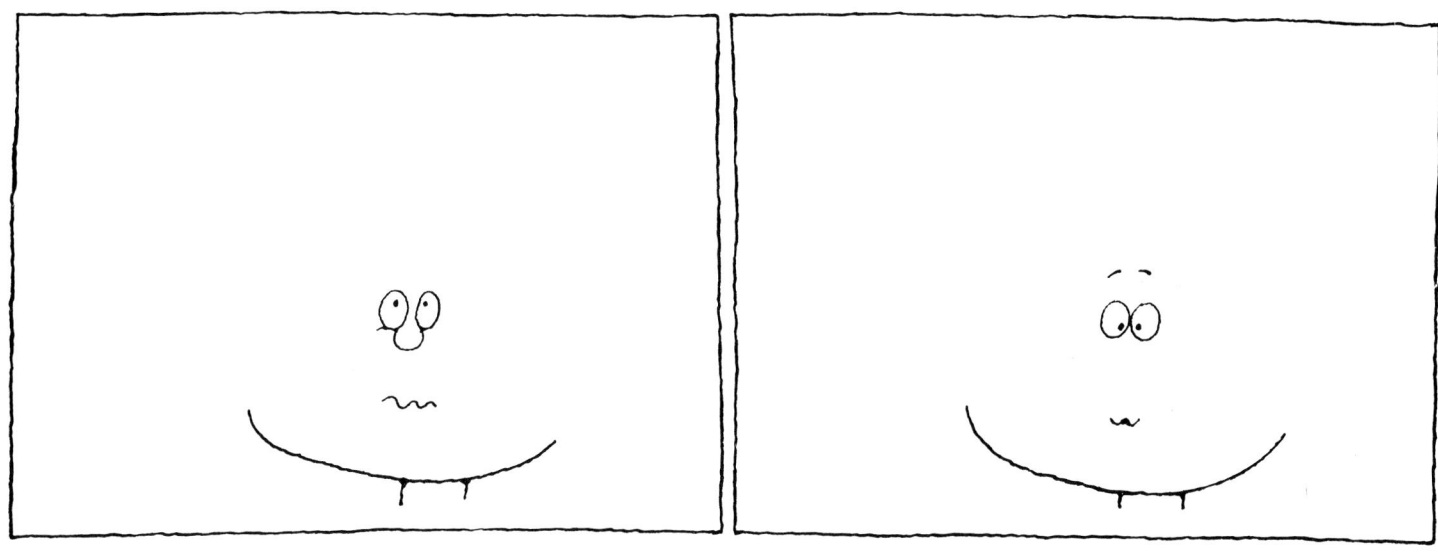

Then he turned blue, and the top of his head grew into strange shapes.

When he turned purple his nose fell off.

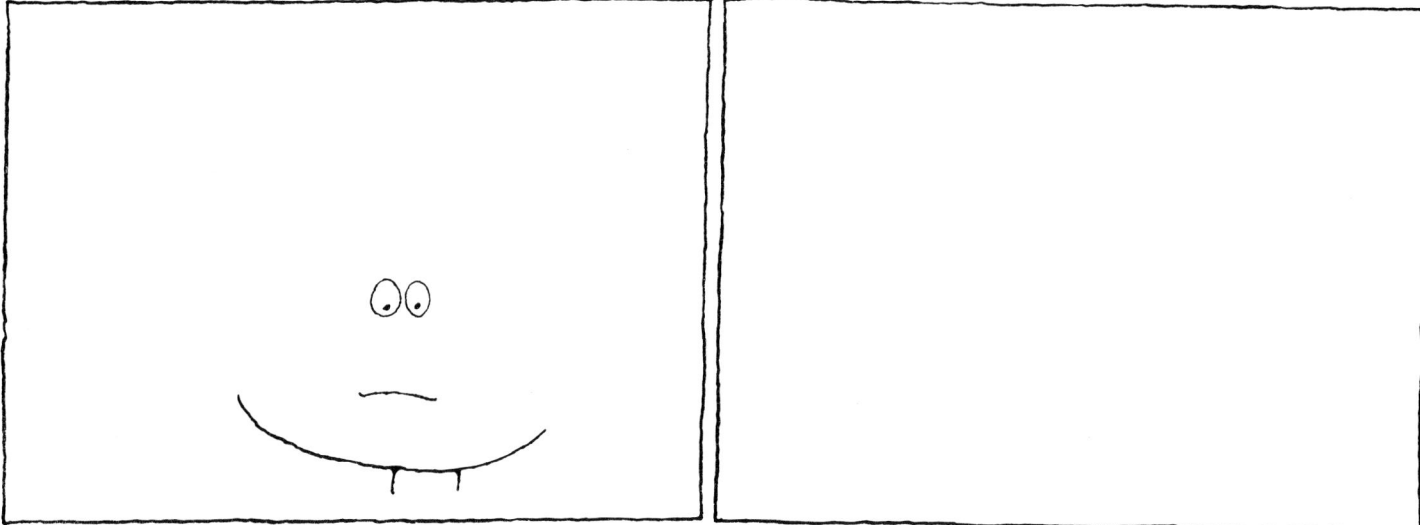

Next he turned red with orange spots, and his teeth started to grow.

What did he look like when the ray gun was switched off?

The Housework machine

This is a helpful housework machine. It can cook, wash dishes, clean the ceiling and feed the cat.

What else can you make it do?

Haircombing machine
Cynthia Bristles has problem hair, so she invented a girl-powered haircombing machine to help her out.

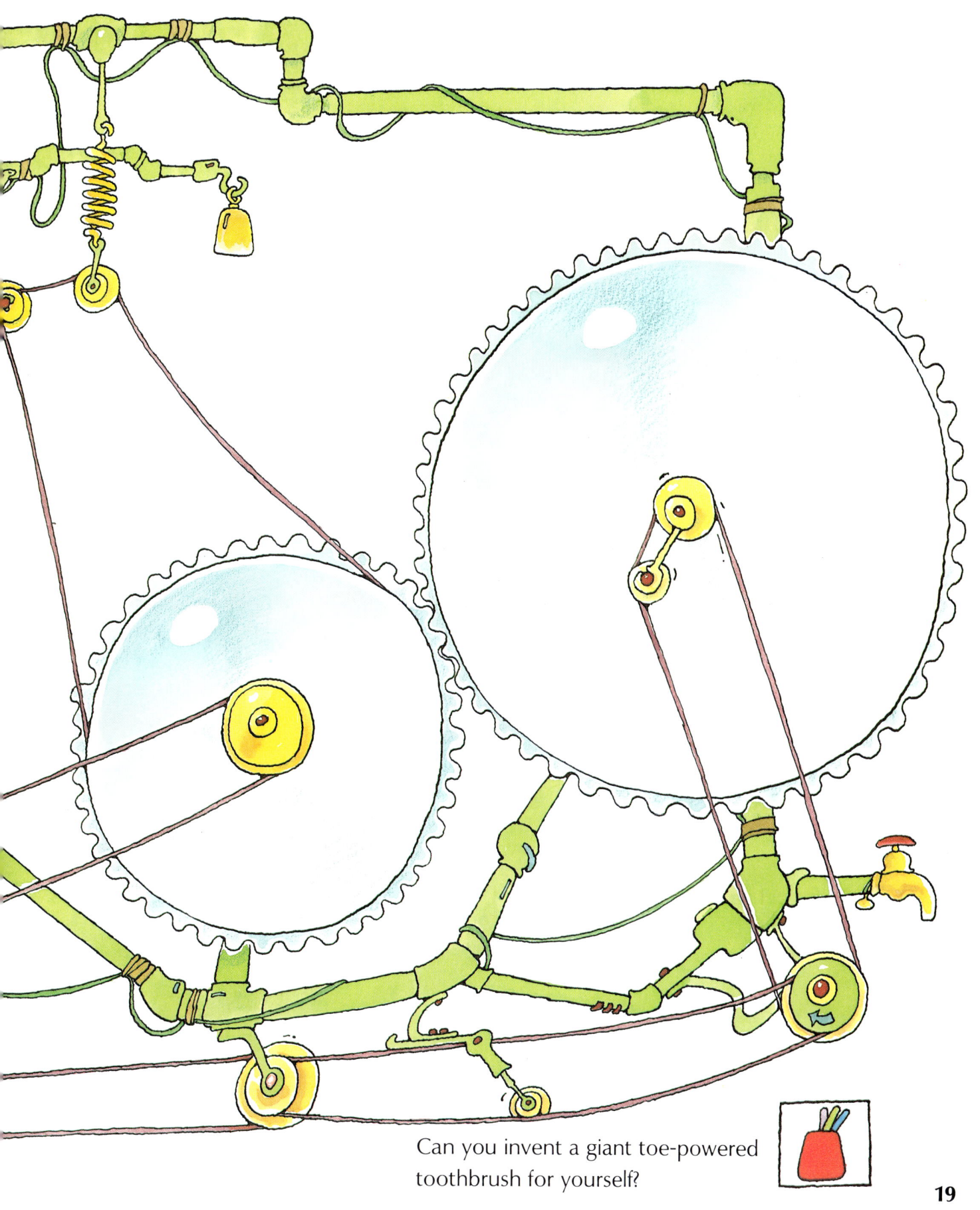

Can you invent a giant toe-powered toothbrush for yourself?

The Giant Submarine

Doctor Fisher loves the sea.
He has built a huge submarine so that he can live underwater.

I have drawn part of the submarine.
Can you draw the rest of it?

Testing machines

A braces-testing machine

What would a shoe-testing machine look like?

A hat tester

Unsuccessful machines

Steam-driven trousers did not catch on because electric trousers were cleaner and quicker.

Steam-driven trousers

This machine did not develop because nobody knew what it did.

Can you draw an even stranger machine?

Machines of the future
Anti-gravity machines that have no wheels

Time machines
You could travel forward in time to find out how you are doing in the future!

Can you draw a machine of the future?